Kindle Fire HD Manual:

The Definitive Kindle Fire HD User Guide

Discover EVERYTHING the new Kindle Fire HD has to offer, including exciting Tips and Tricks, with this Kindle Fire HD Manual

By Francis Monico

Check out Francis Monico's other book for the Kindle Fire HD, outlining his 50 favorite Apps:

Kindle Fire HD Apps: The 50 Top Kindle Fire HD Apps

http://www.amazon.com/Kindle-Fire-HD-Apps-ebook/dp/B00A4CSGDW/

Table of Contents

Chapter 1 - Introduction

Introduction 9

Start Up the Device 9

Getting Registered 10

Exploring Basic Features and Functions 12

The Battery and How to Care for It 13

Let Your Fingers Do the Clicking 14

Chapter 2 – The Kindle Fire HD

The Kindle Fire HD 15

Kindle Fire 1st and 2nd Generation 15

The Kindle eReader Family 16

Versus the Kindle Fire 17

4G Connectivity 17

Cloud Storage Features 19

New Display   20

Dual-Band Wireless   21

Processor and Graphics   21

Expanded Integration of Email and Other Services   22

Productivity   23

Entertainment   24

Skype   26

Amazon Features   27

One-Click   28

Audio   29

Kid Friendly Features and Security   29

Versus the iPad   30

iOS vs. Android   30

App Availability and Control   31

Expanded User Options   31

Price   32

Display   32

Support 32

Shopping Integration 33

Chapter 3 – Technical Aspects

Tech Stuff 34

Hooking Up to a Computer 34

How Have the Controls Changed? 35

Does It Work with All Computers? 35

Wireless Networks vs. 4G 35

Understanding 4G in General 36

Chapter 4 – Basic Use

Basic Use 38

Using the Wireless Dual-Band 38

Tips and Tricks with Networks 39

Downloading/Uploading and the Cloud 39

Downloading Purchased Content 40

Changing Users 40

Security and Restrictions on Use 41

Chapter 5 - Common Frustrations

Common Frustrations 42

Where Did the Keyboard Go? 42

What is HD and Am I Seeing It? 43

Understanding Advanced Audio 43

Locking Someone Out of My Amazon Account 44

Chapter 6 – Care

Care 45

Screen Protectors: Do I Need One? 45

Protecting the Device from Shock 46

Cases 47

Chargers: Are Third-Party Versions Okay? 48

Warranty Terms and Conditions 48

Chapter 7 - Amazon Prime: The Game Changer

Amazon Prime: The Game Changer 50

What Is It? 50

Shipping 51

Movies 51

The Cloud 52

Lending Library 53

Is It Worth It To You? 53

Fees vs. Savings 54

Instant Shopping 54

Full Use of Your Device 55

Chapter 8 - Handy Tips and Tricks

Handy Tips and Tricks 56

Looking for HD Content 56

Get a Stand 56

Explore X-Ray 57

Have Fun with the Audio 57

Explore Apps 58

Conclusion 59

8

Chapter 1

Introduction

Congratulations on purchasing a Kindle Fire HD! Your device is one of the most impressive where the value for the money you spent is concerned. A viable rival for the iPad and other much more expensive eReaders, this device is packed with features and has a screen resolution that puts it on par with devices that cost hundreds of dollars more.

When you receive your Kindle Fire HD, verify that all the parts and accessories are there. If you're missing anything, contact Amazon and let them know. You should have a wall charger included with the package, which you'll use to complete your first charge cycle.

Start Up the Device

Starting up your Kindle Fire HD is easy. The battery will be partially charged when it arrives, but it's a good idea to leave it plugged in overnight before you fire it up so that the battery is fully charged. If you don't have all night, try to let it charge for at least 3 to 4 hours.

TIP: On the new Kindle Fire HD, there is no indicator light on the device to demonstrate if it is fully charged. A workaround for this is to download the app "Battery HD" from the Amazon App store, which will give your devices battery status upon swiping the screen.

When you plug your Kindle Fire HD in, it will turn on automatically. The first screen you see will be the locked screen, which has an arrow on the screen. Drag the arrow across the screen to unlock the device and you'll be brought to the Amazon registration interface.

Getting Registered

You have to register your Kindle Fire HD to take advantage of all the features it includes. This registration gives you a free trial of Amazon Prime, which will be gone into in greater detail later on.

The first step of the registration process involves hooking up to your wireless connection, which the wizard will guide you through. After that, you'll use your username and password from Amazon to complete the registration. You'll get a confirmation email sent to the same address you use for your Amazon account to indicate that the registration process is complete.

If something happens and you're not able to complete the registration process right away, here's how you go back and do it.

1) Tap the Gear Icon at the top right of the screen

2) Select "Wi-Fi"

3) Select your wireless network

4) Fill in the password field

5) When you're connected, the word "connected" will appear to the right of the network name

After you've completed the above procedure:

1) Tap the Gear Icon

2) Select "More"

3) Select "My Account"

4) Fill in the email address and password you use at Amazon.com

You're registered!

Exploring Basic Features and Functions

The Amazon Kindle Fire HD is a big step up from their older models, but many of the features and functionalities remain essentially the same. The Kindle Fire HD runs on the Android operating system, which will be detailed further in a later chapter but, if you have an Android phone, the OS will be somewhat familiar to you.

The important elements that you'll want to keep in mind are as follows:

The Gear Icon allows you to make changes to behind the scenes features such as your wireless network, your Amazon account, your browser preferences and so forth.

The keyboard appears when you tap on any field where text can be entered—email body, search field, etc.

The HDMI connection expands the flexibility of the Amazon Kindle Fire HD tremendously beyond what previous models offered.

Take a look around the device, click on the various sections for movies, music and so forth and just explore. The easiest way to familiarize yourself with this device is to play around with it a bit.

TIP: Your Amazon account is connected to your Kindle Fire HD. Remember that it's easy to make purchases off of the device, so be careful when you're browsing around!

The Battery and How to Care for It

Look around the Internet and you'll find all sorts of conflicting information about battery charging. Your Amazon Kindle Fire HD is powered by a high-quality Lithium Ion battery. Battery "memory"—when the battery only charges to a fraction of its potential if it's charged partially over and over—is not an issue with these batteries.

These batteries do, however, have a limited amount of charge cycles. Fortunately, these batteries have enough capacity to charge that this will not likely be an issue for you at all.

To make sure your battery performs its best, however, most sources recommend the following:

- Discharge the battery to as close as 0% as you can before charging it up

- Leave it plugged in during use to avoid hassles with drained batteries

- Never use any adapter except one designed specifically for this device

- The first time you use the device after the initial charging, discharge the battery completely to condition it

Let Your Fingers Do the Clicking

The Amazon Kindle Fire HD is a touchscreen device. This means that your keyboard and mouse are basically just your fingers. When you want a keyboard, tap in a field where you can enter text.

You can drag and drop just as you would on a computer equipped with a mouse. Tapping on the screen has the same effect as clicking your mouse button. There are single- and double-tap enabled features on these devices.

TIP: If you cannot select something by tapping on it, try using more or less force or holding your finger on the icon for slightly longer.

Chapter 2

The Kindle Fire HD

The Kindle Fire HD is the latest of Amazon's tablet computers. It comes from a long line of high-quality tablets, however, and, like the rest of them, it puts the power of the best tablet computers in the hands of people who don't want to spend a huge amount of money on these devices.

To give you an idea of how the Kindle Fire HD relates to its predecessors, here is a listing of some of the other Kindle products available from Amazon and a comparison between them and your new Kindle Fire HD.

Kindle Fire 1st and 2nd Generation

The Kindle Fire 1st and 2nd Generation tablets were the first full-color, multimedia tablets that Amazon put out. They both feature high-resolution screens and are excellent devices. The Kindle Fire HD's resolution, however, blows them away, making it a better choice for multimedia activities. The Kindle Fire HD is differentiated by its larger screen, its HDMI cable and, of course, its improved processor and storage capacities.

All Kindle Fire devices are tablet computers. This differentiates them from the other part of the Kindle family, the eReaders. Sometimes, it's easier to define a product by its competition. The main competition for the Kindle Fire line of devices is the Apple iPad. Like the iPad, all Kindle Fire devices can run apps, surf the Internet with a browser, provide email access, allow you to play games, read books and much more.

The Kindle eReader Family

This line of devices includes the Kindle, the Kindle Touch, the Kindle Paperwhite and the Kindle Keyboard. These devices have monochrome eInk displays that are optimized for text, though they also display black and white photos very well.

The Kindle eReaders are designed for those who want to read eBooks with minimal distraction and with an interface that is almost identical to reading ink off of a printed page. The Touch and Keyboard devices are differentiated by the former utilizing a touchscreen interface and the latter having an attached keyboard. These devices include the Barnes and Nobles Nook and other eInk readers as among their competition.

Versus the Kindle Fire

There are two versions of the Kindle Fire HD: The 7-inch and the 8.9-inch. The Kindle Fire comes in a 7-inch display model only. Beyond that, here is a breakdown of the basic differences between the devices.

	Kindle Fire	Kindle Fire HD 7	Kindle Fire HD 8.9
Resolution	1024x600	1280x800	1920x1200
Processor	1GHz Dual Core	1.2GHz Dual Core	1.5GHZ Dual Core
Storage	8GB	16 or 32 GB	16,32 or 64GB
Camera	No	Yes, Front	Yes, Front
Input/Output	microUSB	microUSB, microHDMI	microUSB, microHDMI

The Kindle Fire HD is the latest, greatest thing but, as you can see, the Kindle Fire is still a great device. The improvements on the Kindle Fire HD will add a lot for those who wanted something a bit more flexible than the Kindle Fire HD and who wanted something closer to the iPad in functionality and performance.

4G Connectivity

The 8.9" Kindle Fire HD comes with 4G-capability option. The 7' Kindle Fire HD does not. This serves as a backup connection for when you cannot connect to a Wi-Fi network and has some great features of its own. The 4G connection is priced at $50 per year.

This connection allows you to use 20GB of cloud storage through Amazon and you'll get $10 of credit for apps through the Amazon App Store. There is a data cap on the amount of downloading you can do on this connection, however, which is currently set at 250MB. If all of this confuses you a bit, here are some tips for using your 4G connection sensibly.

Streaming music, downloading content or sending files to and taking them from the cloud should be done on a Wi-Fi connection.

If you're worried about the safety of a public Wi-Fi—coffee shop, airport, etc.—do not use the 4G connection to check personal sites such as Facebook and your email.

Think of your 4G connection as a backup. You can turn off 4G connectivity to save on your bandwidth usage by disabling your network connectivity from the Gear Icon.

Your 4G connectivity is provided by AT&T. If you're not happy with the data cap that comes with the device—it is very small, be aware of this—you can purchase a different plan from AT&T for a higher price. Using the Wi-Fi connection, however, is a great way to save on your bandwidth usage.

Cloud Storage Features

The native storage features on the Kindle Fire HD may not seem that extensive, but remember that you have access to the Amazon cloud and that means that you have as much storage as you want to pay for.

You access the cloud storage from the Cloud icon, which appears on the Games, Apps, Books, Music, Videos, Newsstand, Audiobooks, Photos and Docs libraries. To see what you have stored on the cloud, simply tap the icon that says "Cloud". This will give you a listing of the files that you have stored under that category on your cloud storage.

To download anything that you have stored on the cloud, just tap its icon. If you have a lot of content on the Cloud and want to download it to your Kindle more easily, you can do so by connecting the device to your computer and transferring it via USB. This is a bit easier than utilizing the Cloud interface from the Kindle itself. It also avoids any issues with consuming bandwidth.

Remember that you have 20GB to play with just for owning a Kindle Fire HD. If you want more cloud storage, you can buy it from Amazon for a very reasonable rate.

New Display

The display on the Kindle Fire HD is one of its standout features. Any image that you view on this display looks amazingly clear and pixilation is not an issue. You'll only notice the pixilation if you have very good vision and, in this case, "very good" means the type of vision you'd expect someone who pilots jet fighters to have.

The screen's high resolution, to the device's credit, does not slow down the carousel or slider features one bit. This device was designed to be a competitor for the iPad in terms of display quality and, where that is concerned, it does very well.

Video will also be crisp, clean and in real HD—depending upon whether the video you're watching is in that format—so you'll have a great experience watching movies and other videos on the device.

Where text is concerned, there isn't that much difference, simply because text doesn't really require a lot of display power to show up crisp and clean. The device does have the "reader" mode that the Kindle Fire featured, however, which makes webpages appear clearer and more book-like when you're viewing them. Access this by clicking the Glasses icon when you're on a webpage, which shows up when you tap anywhere on the screen.

Dual-Band Wireless

The dual-band wireless is a feature that you'll experience in a behind the scenes way. The Kindle Fire HD supports all of the common wireless network security protocols, including Open, WEP, WPA PSK, WPA2 PSK, WPA EAP and WPA2 EAP. It also supports B, G and N type routers at 2.4GHz. A and N routers on 5GHz are also supported by the device. For most users, this will simply mean that you can connect to any Wi-Fi and that you'll get the full capacity of the network in terms of data transfer rates.

TIP: If your network password is changed, the easiest way to correct it on the Kindle Fire HD is simply to "Forget" the network, which is an option when you're shown the list of available Wi-Fi connections.

Processor and Graphics

All Kindle Fire HD devices have dual-core processors that are more than capable of handling video, music and so forth. You should notice some improvement in speed if you're moving from a 1st or 2nd Generation Kindle Fire.

The graphics on these devices, as noted above, are standout features. Unlike some other devices, the Kindle Fire HD can play most any format of video used on the web, which means that you can not only enjoy the high-quality resolution but that you can utilize just about any technology used to put video into web pages!

Expanded Integration of Email and Other Services

The Kindle Fire HD has the same functionalities that make it easy to access email, social media sites and other personal resources in an improved form compared to the Kindle Fire.

Set up an account first. The process is easy:

1) Go to the Home screen

2) Swipe open the menu at the top of the screen by swiping downward from the top

3) Click on the "More" entry

4) Look for Email, Contacts, Calendars under Amazon Applications and tap on them as needed

5) Tap "Add Account"'

A wizard will appear that guides you through the process of setting up email accounts from any of the major providers. Just select your provider from the list and follow the directions.

To check email with the Email App:

1) Go to your Home screen

2) Tap on Apps

3) Tap on the Email App

The commands for the Email App are intuitive. To respond to a message, click "Respond", for instance. The only feature that is not apparent is the option to refresh the inbox, which is found under the Menu Icon on the device.

The Kindle Fire HD can handle multiple email accounts. You'll have to choose which one is your default provider, however. If you don't have one of the listed accounts, you can set up your access manually.

Productivity

You can purchase applications for your Kindle Fire HD that allow you to use it as a productivity tool. Keep in mind, however, that this device gets its highest marks for its entertainment value and because it offers easy access to communications such as emails and social media.

There are several different apps that you might want to try for your Kindle. They include OfficeSuite professional, which is a popular office option. There are other ways that these devices can be used for productivity.

Whiteboard Pro, for instance, allows you to draw and erase on your device as you would on a regular whiteboard. There are applications available that allow you to view documents but not edit them, as well, which makes the Kindle Fire HD great for reviewing documents and other materials.

The Kindle Fire HD doesn't offer much for some office tasks, such as being used as a word processor, but it's great for presentations, for communication and for some other office purposes.

Calendar options are numerous and many are free.

Entertainment

Entertainment is where the Kindle Fire HD really shines. The default interface gives you access to various content sections, which allows you to download, access and enjoy many different types of entertainment and informational content. From the Home screen, you'll see the following sections.

- Newsstand

- Books

- Music

- Video

- Docs

- Apps

- Web

These sections all contain exactly what their names imply. On each of these sections, you'll find a toggle that allows you to switch between "Cloud" and "Device". The highlighted selection indicates whether you're looking at content that is stored on your device or content that is stored in the Amazon Cloud. To move one to the other, press and hold the icon and select the appropriate option from the menu that comes up.

The Kindle Fire HD is set up to make moving, accessing and buying new content as easy as possible. If you want something new to add to your library, just click on the section and select "Store". You'll have the option to buy a lot of content and, if you have Amazon Prime—which you will for a free trial, at least—you can stream content directly to your device.

Skype

Skype has a lot of potential for having fun and for productivity. The messenger is nicely integrated with the Android operating system and Kindle makes it easy to use.

Your Kindle Fire HD—either model—has a camera on the front that you can use to video chat with friends. Remember, however, that you'll want to do this on Wi-Fi connections only, unless you're not at all worried about consuming 4G bandwidth.

Here's how to set it up:

1) Go to the Home Screen

2) Go to Apps

3) Switch to the Cloud

4) Tap on Skype and let it download

5) The download is complete when you see a checkmark by the App

6) Tap Skype

7) Check your Apps library and go to the Device tab. You'll see Skype

You can either sign into an existing Skype account or make a new one.

TIP: You can use Skype to call telephone numbers—including international numbers—with your Kindle Fire HD.

Your camera will turn on for you when you make video calls. You can make audio-only calls, as well. The microphone is built into your Kindle Fire HD.

You can buy credit to call telephones from Skype. You can add other features, as well.

Amazon Features

Most of the Amazon features that come with your Kindle are so tightly integrated into the device that using them is just a matter of course. What will define your experience is really whether or not you subscribe to Amazon Prime. If you do, you can watch a huge number of videos for free that you'd have to rent otherwise, for instance. The Cloud feature is among the most notable features.

When you're in any of your libraries—Music, Video, etc.—be sure you check to see whether or not you're looking at the cloud or your device. You can access your cloud storage by simply logging into your Amazon account, as well, and you'll have full access to all of your files. For Amazon content, your cloud storage quota is unlimited.

Cloud storage is also going to be the best bet for storing all of your media files. Your device can have up to 64GB of onboard storage, but using the cloud ensures that your data is backed up, that you have access to it from anywhere and that you can store far more data than you could on your device.

One-Click

If you're sharing your device with others, be sure you're aware of your one-click purchasing option. They could end up buying something without meaning to. The best and most reliable way to turn off one-click shopping is to do it from your amazon account page.

1) Go to Amazon.com

2) Sign in

3) Click on "Your Account"

4) Click on "1-Click Settings"

5) Turn off the option for 1-Click Ordering

Shopping for anything on the Kindle Fire HD is so easy that you may just want to skip 1-Click. The store is readily accessible from the Library pages and purchasing is very fast and convenient.

Audio

The Kindle Fire HD has the same 3.5mm audio jack that you'll find on most tablet computers. This can be used to listen with headphones, as an output jack for speakers or, if you want, you can even hook this up to a vehicles MP3 input to play music.

The Kindle Fire HD also has built-in stereo speakers, so you don't have to haul around an extra piece of equipment if you want to listen when you're on the go. The sound is Dolby stereo, so you'll be able to get great sound out of the device if you hook it up to speakers or headphones.

Kid Friendly Features and Security

There are a lot of kid-friendly features on the Amazon Kindle Fire HD. There is, for instance, an entire section of the App store that's designed for kids.

If you want to make sure that your kids aren't making purchases or doing other things with the Kindle that you don't want them doing, you can go to the Parental Controls options.

1) Open the Gear Icon

2) Tap "More"

3) Tap "Parental Controls"

4) Select your desired options.

Versus the iPad

The Kindle Fire HD is a direct competitor for the Apple iPad line of products. The Apple iPad products are not tied into Amazon the way the Kindle is, but are tied into Apple. There are some notable differences that may make you glad that you got the less expensive Kindle Fire HD.

iOS vs. Android

iOS is from Apple and Android is from Google. They're both mobile operating systems used in a variety of devices. The Kindle Fire HD uses the Android operating system. This offers you some advantages over iOS.

- Highly customizable interface

- Freedom to get out of Amazon Home interface

- Many apps

- Apps are not tightly controlled

App Availability and Control

Android operating system devices pretty much allows you to install any app you want on your device. The Amazon App store is set up to be the default app provider for your device, but you can get around it with a bit of work and with some learning about how Android works.

On iPad devices, you are completely restricted to whatever apps Apple has approved for their device and have to "jailbreak" the device if you would prefer to make your own decisions about apps.

Expanded User Options

Apple places tight controls over what you're allowed to do with their devices. Android OS devices do not have these restrictions and customizing these is really quite easy. It's done with apps, such as Go Launcher.

Price

The price difference between the two devices is usually around $200, the iPad being the more expensive option. This changes, of course, but the Kindle Fire HD will likely appeal to those individuals who don't want to spend $500 or more getting a device used mostly for entertainment.

Display

The iPad devices do have larger displays than the Kindle Fire HD. The crispness of the image, however, is roughly equivalent, according to most reviews and the HD gets excellent feedback in this regard.

Support

Amazon and Apple both have highly regarded support options for their devices. Amazon's options on their website include a great deal of written documentation and videos.

Shopping Integration

The Kindle Fire HD excels in this regard. In addition to being tightly integrated with the Amazon store, which allows you to get video and audio, as well as other materials, very easily, you have the Amazon Prime option. There is no equivalent of Amazon Prime where the iPad is concerned.

The Apple iPad is one of the most highly regarded tablet devices on the market, but the Amazon Kindle Fire HD is a strong competitor. The main difference that tends to attract people to the Kindle is the price and the easy integration with Amazon's vast library of content.

Chapter 3

Tech Stuff

You can rest assured that the Amazon Kindle Fire HD is not a device that you'll need a lot of technical expertise to operate. It's straightforward, the connection options are very easy to understand and there's nothing very difficult required of you. Here are some of the basics that you should master.

Hooking Up to a Computer

Utilizing the microUSB connection, you can hook up to a computer and access the Kindle directly as another drive. You'll see the appropriate directories for all of your libraries listed under the drive letter that applies, which will vary from computer to computer.

To connect of disconnect from a computer, swipe the top menu down from the home screen—top of the screen, swipe straight down—and hit the "Connect" or "Disconnect" option, whichever applies.

Your device will connect automatically when you hook it up to USB connection.

TIP: USB 2.0 or 3.0 make transferring files much faster.

How Have the Controls Changed?

There have been minimal changes to any of the controls between the Kindle Fire and Kindle Fire HD devices. If you had a Kindle Fire before, you'll find everything to be essentially the same on the Kindle Fire HD.

Does It Work with All Computers?

Yes. You can hook your device up to a Mac computer with the microUSB cord and access the Kindle volume right from the usual desktop. Linux users will have to go through a much more complicated series of steps to get the device to interface with their computer, depending upon which distribution of Linux they're using.

Wireless Networks vs. 4G

The basics of the 4G connectivity on this device have been covered, but the differences between these two wireless options should be discussed. For most users, the difference is going to come down to money and security.

Public Wi-Fi networks can be very dangerous. People can snoop on your traffic if you're connected to the same Wi-Fi that they are. For this reason, if you're in a public place and you need to use your Kindle to access email, to buy something online or to do something else that requires exchanging personal information, you may want to use the 4G connection. It will be slower and it will consume your allotted bandwidth, but it's generally more secure.

Wi-Fi is the best option when you're at home or on a trusted network. Using your Wi-Fi connection, you can make Skype calls and video calls, you can shop, stream video, stream music and do just about anything else you'd do online.

The general rule is if what you're doing consumes a lot of bandwidth, such as streaming content; make sure that you're on a Wi-Fi and not your 4G connection.

Understanding 4G in General

Your 4G connection is provided by AT&T, so your network availability will be dependent upon what that carrier has in your area. 4G is the latest wireless network technology used for smartphones and other devices. It is faster than 3G but the network for it isn't as extensive. That will change, of course, as it overtakes 3G.

Your 4G access is limited by the amount you purchase every month. The first year, however, allows you the 250GB per month for 1 year. As a reference, an average movie is around 1G in size, so you should not use this feature for streaming or downloading any sizeable content.

Some apps will automatically access your network, such as email apps. Be sure you have your network connection turned off when you go out and about.

Chapter 4

Basic Use

The very basic elements of using your Amazon Kindle Fire HD have been covered, but here are instructions that will guide you through many of the processes that you'll use with the device.

Using the Wireless Dual Band

1) Tap the Gear Icon

2) Tap "More"

3) Select "Wireless Network"

4) Verify that "Wireless Network" is set to "On"

5) Click on the name of the network you want

6) Enter your password

7) Click "Connect"

The dual-band features take care of themselves. The device will default to match your connection's type.

Tips and Tricks with Networks

Inevitably, there will be a problem with your connectivity. This happens with any electronic device. Here are some tips that you can use to remedy these problems when they arise.

- Connection Dropped: Check your Wi-Fi settings to see if the network still shows up. If not, try rebooting your device. Failing that, reboot your wireless router.

- Cannot See Network: Try rebooting your router and turning the Wi-Fi connection on your Kindle off and back on.

- Password Rejected: There is an option on the password entry window for you to show the password. Select that option to make certain that you're typing everything correctly.

Downloading/Uploading and the Cloud

One of the things that you may find confusing about the Kindle Fire HD is where the cloud is located. The cloud is actually accessed by selecting the option from any of your Library screens. Tapping on the icon that says "Cloud" will give you access to any of the content you have stored on the Amazon cloud.

Remember that storing Amazon content on the cloud is free, so you want to take advantage of that to keep your Kindle from filling up with files.

Downloading Purchased Content

If you purchase content that ends up being stored on the Cloud and you want to download it to the device, simply tap and hold your finger on the appropriate icon. You'll be given the option to transfer the content to your device.

Changing Users

The Kindle HD is connected to your Amazon account. The registration process is easy.

1) Tap the Gear Icon

2) Select "More"

3) Select "My Account"

4) Fill in the information

If you decide you want to change the user of the device, go back to the "My Account" menu and select the option to do register the device. The device will be reregistered to whoever enters their Amazon credentials.

Security and Restrictions on Use

Even though they're called parental controls, the "Parental Controls" options on the device allow you to secure it against people using it in ways that could end up costing you money. Go to the Gear Icon and select "More". Select Parental Controls, which will give you all the options you need to lock down your device.

If you find yourself in the unhappy situation of having locked down your device with the parental controls and then having forgotten your password, you can simply reset the device to get everything back to how it was.

Chapter 5

Common Frustrations

Tablet devices have revolutionized how people interact with the Internet and entertain themselves, but they do come with their headaches, as well. Most of them are simply part of the learning curve that's unavoidable when you switch from using a device that uses a keyboard and mouse for your input methods to one that utilizes a touchscreen. Here are some things that you may have to deal with at some point and how to remedy them.

Where Did the Keyboard Go?

One of the most common frustrations occurs when the keyboard disappears as you're typing something. This is pretty easy to remedy. Simply tap in a field where you could enter text. It doesn't matter what kind of a field it is, as long as you can type the word in. This should make the keyboard reappear.

You may run into pages where you cannot get the cursor in a field. You can enlarge the page by spreading your fingers outward from the field that you want to enter text into. This will sometimes allow you to place the cursor in the field more easily and, thereby, give you access to the keyboard.

On the bottom left of the keyboard you will find a button that lets you switch between the QWERTY keyboard, the numerical keyboard and the symbols keyboard. Toggle keyboards by tapping this key.

What is HD and Am I Seeing It?

Videos will indicate whether they are presented in HD. Not all movies will be. If the video itself is not in the HD format, your Kindle device will not be able to display it in HD, either. Your Kindle automatically shows movies that are presented in HD in that format.

HD is remarkably sharp compared to lesser resolutions. Generally speaking, when you're watching something on HD, you'll be aware of it.

Understanding Advanced Audio

The audio on the Kindle Fire HD is Dolby stereo and the speakers are tuned for it. That being said, remember that these are very small speakers, so don't expect them to knock the door off your apartment. The device can be hooked up to external speakers, however, and you'll get excellent sound reproduction. This device has gotten great reviews for its sound capabilities.

Bluetooth is also included on the device, so that can be used to hook up to audio output devices that are compatible with it, as well.

The Kindle Fire HD also comes with the ability to provide text to speech access to books and other written content. In most cases, you'll find that the built-in speakers are more than adequate for giving you sound reproduction that's appropriate for this type of content.

To get the most out of your audio experience when you're watching movies, listening to music or doing something else that's audio intensive, you want to use a good pair of headphones or hook up the device to external speakers.

Locking Someone Out of My Amazon Account

The Kindle Fire HD is tied to your Amazon account, so actually locking somebody out of it is difficult. The best way to do this is to follow the instructions for setting the parental controls up and to make certain that you have disabled one click purchasing on your account.

Chapter 6

Care

The Amazon Kindle Fire HD is a sturdy device, but any electronic device can be damaged. The most dangerous things to your Kindle are water and shock. You'll also want to make certain that you don't allow the screen to get scratched. Here are some tips for keeping your Kindle safe.

Screen Protectors: Do I Need One?

You'll find conflicting advice about whether or not to use screensavers online. Screensavers can protect your device against being scratched, which is important, considering that the screen on this device is one of its standout features.

Applying a screen protector can actually be a bit frustrating. Especially on a device with a screen that is seven inches or larger, you're going to find it difficult to get the screen protector on without having air bubbles trapped underneath it.

One way to improve your luck at this is to utilize a piece of masking tape. Use the masking tape to pull small pieces of dust away from the back of the screen protector by placing their adhesive sides together and gently peeling away the masking tape.

Screen protectors do an excellent job of protecting your screen against damage but among the features that have become very impressive with any tablet device is the fact that the glass on these devices is incredibly durable and scratch resistant.

Utilizing one of the microfiber cloths used to clean lenses will generally give you great results for getting your fingerprints and getting other debris off the screen. Whether or not you want to put a screen protector on the device is up to you, but some people strongly advocate doing it.

Protecting the Device from Shock

Shock refers to any force applied to your Kindle that is not expected and that is generally rather severe. This would come from dropping the device, dropping something on to the device or bumping it against a wall or the arm of the chair when you're moving around.

If you're not going to use a case, make certain that you at least take some measures to protect your device. Set it on the center of the table, rather than on the edge. If you end up browsing on the device before you go to bed or doze off on the couch, make certain that you don't put it on the floor. A little bit of common sense will go a long way toward preventing a disaster.

If you're carrying your Kindle in your backpack or in another bag, be aware of any other objects in that bag that may damage it. Even though these devices are very sturdy, they can be damaged and, in some cases, that damage may be enough to render them useless.

Cases

The best way to prevent your Kindle Fire HD from becoming damaged due to shock is to have it in a sturdy case. This will prevent it from being damaged by objects that fall onto it and from being damaged when it is dropped, which you should assume is going to happen at some point.

Cases for these devices can be very expensive. In fact, because the price of the Amazon Kindle Fire HD is so low, you could conceivably spend a quarter or even half of the price you pay for the device on a good case. Remember that inexpensive cases can provide a lot of shock protection, as well. Look for one that is resistant to water and other liquids – leather, nylon and other materials are all good options in this regard – and look for one that you can fasten the device into firmly so that it does not fall out.

Some cases come with folders and spaces for pens and other materials built into them. Remember that anything you put in one of these cases is likely to end up scratching the screen on your Kindle, so you may want to avoid these types of cases.

Chargers: Are Third-Party Versions Okay?

Chargers are denoted by the type of connections they have, the voltage they deliver, and their current. Provided a charger matches the original charger that came with your device in all these regards, it should work fine.

If you're going to purchase a third-party charger for your Amazon Kindle, you may want to look for one that specifically says it is made for and Amazon Kindle Fire HD. This will ensure that you're getting exactly what you expect.

Warranty Terms and Conditions

The Kindle Fire HD comes with a one-year limited warranty. If there was something genuinely wrong with the device, Amazon will generally replace it for you with little hassle. Go to

Amazon.com/support to find out how to return your device, if necessary.

Be aware of the fact that some activities and uses for the device will void your warranty. Any apps that you download for the device will be warranty by the manufacturer. This is one reason to be wary of apps and to make certain that they come from a good developer before you go ahead and install them on your Kindle Fire.

Chapter 7

Amazon Prime - The Game Changer

Amazon gives you a free trial of Amazon Prime when you purchase a Kindle device. This membership comes with quite a few benefits, particularly for those who order many items from the Amazon website. In addition to this, there are features of Amazon prime that make it ideal for Kindle owners.

The Kindle Fire HD is designed to be a multimedia machine and, to that end, many of the features of Amazon Prime are designed to provide you with easy and inexpensive access to multimedia content to enjoy on your device. Here are the basics of Amazon Prime.

What Is It?

Amazon Prime is a membership program that gives you access to movies and television shows, Kindle books, expedited shipping at no cost and discounts on many of the items sold on the site.

For most users, the savings they will receive will easily offset the cost of the program. If you end up using your Kindle Fire

HD to watch movies and television shows a lot, you'll find that the savings will likely be substantial.

Shipping

Amazon Prime members get free two-day shipping on many of the items available in the Amazon store. In order to figure out whether or not any item is eligible, all you have to do is look at the product page. If it is available under the terms of Amazon Prime, an icon will tell you.

Movies

Just about everybody who gets a Kindle Fire HD is going to want to watch movies on it. After all, the quality of the screen is designed to make this as enjoyable as possible.

Amazon Prime allows you to select from thousands of different movies and television shows and to stream them to your Kindle device for free. Even more, you can stream them to your computer or any other device that can accommodate the feature, as well.

The Kindle Fire HD can be used to rent movies. One of the biggest differences between using this feature with Amazon

Prime and without is that many of the rental movies will be available to you at no cost.

For most people who enjoy watching movies, this feature makes Amazon Prime worth it alone. After all, consider how much the average family spent on renting movies in the days of video stores and compare that to having access to literally thousands of movies for $79 per year.

Videos that are eligible to be watched under these terms are denoted as Prime Instant Videos.

The Cloud

The cloud storage feature doesn't require you to be an Amazon prime member to access it. You get five gigabytes of free storage automatically. You can buy more storage, however, and utilize that to store any media that you purchase from a source other than Amazon.

Keep in mind, however, that Amazon content doesn't eat up any of your cloud storage allocation. You can access the cloud from a desktop computer.

Lending Library

Believe it or not, Amazon was once really nothing more than an online bookstore. It is still one of the biggest and best online bookstores in the world and, as a feature of Amazon Prime, you get access to thousands of e-book titles for free. It functions like a lending library, allowing you to access this content for a limited amount of time.

When you're browsing through the "Books" section of your Library, you'll see that there is an entry to the right of the books listed that allows you to access the Kindle Owner's Lending Library.

This will provide you with access to the extensive collection of e-books that are available to Kindle owners alone. Again, for an avid reader, this feature would likely pay for the entire Amazon Prime membership fee within a year.

Is It Worth It To You?

Whether or not Amazon Prime is worth it to you will depend upon your habits. For the vast majority of users, however, the service does tend to end up paying for itself. Here are some of the reasons why.

Fees vs. Savings

Once you've read a book or watched a movie, there's really no reason other than nostalgia to have a physical copy of it or even a digital copy of it on your device. Reading books available from the Kindle Owner's Lending Library or watching movies that are Prime eligible enables you to get that content whenever you want without actually having to pay a separate fee for it.

If you watch a lot of movies or if you read a lot of books – or both – you'll generally find that $79 per year is not a large fee to pay and that it's probably less than you would pay to purchase or rent those items separately.

Instant Shopping

Amazon designed the Kindle devices, in part, as content delivery systems. When you purchase a movie on Amazon, you can watch it on your device instantly. When you purchase an album, you can plug in your headphones or external speakers and crank it up to your heart's delight.

Amazon Prime offers enough of a discount on such purchases that the savings combined with the instant delivery of the content make it more than worth the fee.

Full Use of Your Device

Some of the features in the Amazon Prime membership are specifically designed for Kindle users. If you're not using them, you're not really getting the full usage out of your device.

Being able to stream movies instantly, to read books without having to pay for them and other features are all great ways to enhance the usefulness of your device and to ensure that you get the maximum amount of enjoyment out of it.

Amazon Prime really is a game changer, just as the title of this chapter implies. Because it is so useful, there's really no reason to cheat yourself out of what it has to offer and, if you want to make certain that you are enjoying your Kindle as much as possible, you really should not go without a membership to Prime.

Chapter 8

Handy Tips and Tricks

The following information is included just as a bonus to help you get a bit more usage out of your Kindle Fire HD. Even though it's much less expensive than the competing tablets on the market, it's still not exactly cheap and you want to make sure you enjoy it as much as possible. Here are some ways that you can do just that.

Look for HD Content

If you haven't had an HD device before, there was probably no point in you looking for HD content to watch. Start keeping an eye out for it. Look for movies and television shows that are available in HD. You will most certainly notice the difference and, once you get used to it, you'll be very aware when a movie or television show is not shown in HD.

Get a Stand

Your Kindle Fire HD is likely to become one of your favorite travel companions. Get a stand for it so that you can stand it up on tables and watch it when you're on the road in hotel rooms or at other locations.

Some of the cases available have built in stands, and these are great features to have. Not only are they good for watching movies and television, they're excellent if you want to use your Kindle Fire HD for productivity tasks, such as giving presentations.

Explore X-Ray

X-Ray is a great feature that's included with Kindle. It allows you to get additional information on any content that you're watching. Tap the screen to access this feature when you're watching a movie or television show. If you're having arguments about who is in the movie or what other movies they were in, this is a great way to find out.

Have Fun with the Audio

Dolby stereo sound is nothing to scoff at. It gives excellent audio reproduction. Make certain that you're getting the most out of it. By hooking your Kindle Fire HD up to external speakers, you can utilize equalizers and other enhancing devices to get a better sound quality out of the device.

Make certain that you get good headphones, as well. The cheap ear bud type headphones that are widely available seldom have good sound reproduction, particularly at the low end of the spectrum. Get good headphones and enjoy the quality audio that you paid for.

Explore Apps

Remember that your Kindle Fire HD is far more than a shopping device for Amazon. Look at some of the Android applications available and see how they might expand the functionality of your device and make it more fun. Unlike other companies, Amazon doesn't mind if you customize your device into exactly what you want!

Conclusion

The Kindle Fire HD will be a familiar device to anybody who had a Kindle Fire or a similar tablet computer. Remember that this device, however, has been greatly expanded in terms of its capabilities and that its interconnection with Amazon Prime makes it a truly remarkable multimedia machine!

CPSIA information can be obtained at www.ICGtesting.com
Printed in the USA
LVOW10s1508290915

456191LV00021B/1390/P